EASY DOUGHNUT COOKBOOK

THE EF.

By
BookSumo Press
Copyright © 2015 by Saxonberg Associates
All rights reserved

Published by
BookSumo, a division of Saxonberg Associates
http://www.booksumo.com/

INTRODUCTION

Welcome to *The Effortless Chef Series*! Thank you for taking the time to download the *Easy Doughnut Cookbook*. Come take a journey with me into the delights of easy cooking. The point of this cookbook and all my cookbooks is to exemplify the effortless nature of cooking simply.

In this book we focus on tasty and delicious doughnuts! After you read all the recipes you will realized how simple these tasty treats actually are. Also some of the recipes may be a bit on the longer side, but do not worry they are still super simple. You will find that even though the recipes are simple, the taste of the dishes is quite amazing.

So lets jump in and start cooking.

TABLE OF CONTENTS

Introduction 2
Table of Contents 3
Legal Notes 5
    Easy Classical Doughnut I 6
    Easy Doughnuts of Buttermilk 9
    Classical Doughnuts of Applesauce I
    13
    Classical Herman Doughnuts I 17
    Doughnuts In Poland 21
    Doughnuts From Canada 25
    Super Simple Doughnuts with Jelly 29
    A Simple Doughnut of Yeast 33
    A Muffin That Is A Doughnut Too ... 37
    A Doughnut From Cake Mix 41
    Oven Doughnuts 45
    Delightful Cream Based Doughnuts 48
    A Jelly Cupcake Doughnut 53
    Doughnuts from Greenland 56

A Strawberry Shortcake Sweet Doughnut 59
Jelly Doughnut II 62
Doughnut Ice Cream 65
Bread Pudding Doughnuts Re-Imagined 68
Herman Doughnuts II 71
Classical Doughnuts with Apple Cider 74
Oven Doughnuts II 78
Classical Doughnuts with Apple Cider II 81
Doughnuts in the Netherlands 85
Doughnuts for Autumn 88
(Maple and Pumpkin) 88

LEGAL NOTES

ALL RIGHTS RESERVED. NO PART OF THIS BOOK MAY BE REPRODUCED OR TRANSMITTED IN ANY FORM OR BY ANY MEANS. PHOTOCOPYING, POSTING ONLINE, AND / OR DIGITAL COPYING IS STRICTLY PROHIBITED UNLESS WRITTEN PERMISSION IS GRANTED BY THE BOOK'S PUBLISHING COMPANY. LIMITED USE OF THE BOOK'S TEXT IS PERMITTED FOR USE IN REVIEWS WRITTEN FOR THE PUBLIC AND/OR PUBLIC DOMAIN.

Easy Classical Doughnut I

Ingredients:

- 2 quarts oil for deep frying
- 1 (10 ounce) can refrigerated buttermilk biscuit dough
- 1 cup confectioners' sugar

Directions

- Get a deep pan, good for frying or a deep fryer and set its temperature to 375 degrees F with oil in it.
- Now grab your biscuit mix and take them apart, take some time to create a hole in the biscuit so that it is doughnut like. But understand that you can fashion your biscuits in any style.
- Take your cut biscuits and enter them into the frying pan or deep fryer. Let the doughnuts cook until they are fried golden on each side.
- Now it is important to remove your doughnuts from the oil and let them dry and drain.

- Now take your sugar and cover the doughnuts with the sugar. The best way to do this is to place your sugar inside of a container and then place the individual doughnut into the container and move the doughnut about, until it is covered in sugar.

Serving Size: 8 servings

Timing Information:

Preparation	Cooking	Total Time
10 mins	10 mins	20 mins

Nutritional Information:

Calories	366 kcal
Carbohydrates	30.1 g
Cholesterol	< 1 mg
Fat	26.8 g
Fiber	< 1%
Protein	2.3 g
Sodium	350 mg

* Percent Daily Values are based on a 2,000 calorie diet.

Easy Doughnuts of Buttermilk

Ingredients:

- 2 cups vegetable oil for frying

Doughnuts:

- 2 cups buttermilk
- 1 cup white sugar
- 2 large eggs, beaten
- 5 cups sifted all-purpose flour
- 2 tsps baking soda
- 1 tsp baking powder
- 1 tsp salt
- 1 tsp ground nutmeg
- 1/4 tsp ground cinnamon
- 1/2 cup melted butter

Glaze:

- 3 cups confectioners' sugar
- 1 tbsp margarine, softened (optional)
- 1/2 tsp vanilla extract
- 2 tbsps milk, or as needed

Directions

- To being this recipe we need to start with a large pan that will be good for frying, or possibly a deep fryer.
- Place oil into this pan and get it to a temperature of 375 degree Fahrenheit
- Now grab a container good for mixing and combine the following ingredients: eggs, buttermilk, and white sugar.
- Get another mixing container (possibly a bowl) and combine the following ingredients: cinnamon, flour, nutmeg, baking soda, salt, and baking powder.
- You now want to combine the two sets of contents into one and also mix in some butter. Continue to knead this mixture until you have dough.
- Now cover a place for rolling with flour.
- Roll out your dough until it is 1/4 inch in thickness. Now grab a doughnut cutting device of about 2 and a half inches and cut some treats.

- Now grab another container for mixing and combine the following ingredients until you find that they are smooth: vanilla extract, sugar, and margarine. While mixing these together you want to slowly work in some milk, until you get a mixture that is frosty and glaze like for your doughnuts.
- Take a group of uncooked doughnuts and place them into your fryer or pan of hot oil and fry them for about one minute on each side.
- Once each doughnut has been fried for one minute you want to put them aside to rest and drain off any extra oil.
- After the doughnuts are dried take the glaze and cover each evenly.
- Enjoy.

Serving Size: 36 servings

Timing Information:

Preparation	Cooking	Total Time
20 mins	5 mins	25 mins

Nutritional Information:

Calories	172 kcal
Carbohydrates	30 g
Cholesterol	18 mg
Fat	4.7 g
Fiber	0.5 g
Protein	2.7 g
Sodium	189 mg

* Percent Daily Values are based on a 2,000 calorie diet.

CLASSICAL DOUGHNUTS OF APPLESAUCE I

Ingredients:

- 2 quarts oil for deep frying
- 3/4 cup white sugar
- 2 tbsps butter, softened
- 2 eggs
- 3/4 cup applesauce
- 4 cups sifted all-purpose flour
- 2 tsps baking powder
- 1 tsp salt
- 1/2 tsp baking soda
- 1/2 tsp ground mace
- 1/2 tsp ground cinnamon
- 1/2 cup buttermilk
- 1/4 cup confectioners' sugar for dusting

Directions

- To being this recipe we need to start with a large pan that will be good for frying, or possibly a deep fryer.

- Place oil into this pan and get it to a temperature of 375 degree Fahrenheit
- Now grab a container good for mixing and combine the following ingredients: applesauce, sugar, eggs, and butter. Get another bowl and combine the following ingredients as well: cinnamon, flour, mace, baking powder, baking soda, and salt
- Take both mixtures and combine them together and form a dough before continuing. While stirring both mixtures to form dough while slowly mixing in some buttermilk.
- Cover a work surface with some flour and roll out your dough into a layer that is about 1 inch in thickness.
- Get your doughnut cutting device and cut some doughnuts out.
- Put a batch of uncooked doughnuts into the hot oil and cook them on one side until you find that they are floating to the top of the oil this should take about 1 minute of frying but may be longer. Once the doughnut is

floating flip it and continue frying until both sides are golden.
- Let the doughnuts sit and drain before you cover them with sugar.
- Enjoy.

Serving Size: 2 dozen

Timing Information:

Preparation	Cooking	Total Time
30 mins	20 mins	50 mins

Nutritional Information:

Calories	190 kcal
Carbohydrates	24.7 g
Cholesterol	18 mg
Fat	9 g
Fiber	0.7 g
Protein	2.9 g
Sodium	172 mg

* Percent Daily Values are based on a 2,000 calorie diet.

Classical Herman Doughnuts I

Ingredients:

- 8 cups vegetable oil (for frying)
- 3 tbsps shortening
- 1/2 cup white sugar
- 2 eggs, beaten
- 1 cup Herman Sourdough Starter
- 1/2 cup milk
- 2 cups all-purpose flour
- 1 tsp baking soda
- 1/2 tsp salt
- 1/4 tsp ground nutmeg
- 2 tbsps confectioners' sugar

Directions

- Get a large container good for mixing and combine the following ingredients: sugar and shortening (work these into a cream like mixture), and also mix in some milk and Herman starter.
- Grab another container for mixing and combine the

following ingredients: nutmeg, flour, and baking soda.
- Now you want to combine both mixtures to create your delicious doughnut dough.
- Cover a working area with some flour and begin to flatten your dough out into a sheet that should be about half an inch thick.
- Use your doughnut cutting device to cut out some doughnuts.
- For this type of doughnut you want to let them sit for about one hr, while covered with cloth.
- After an hour of sitting you should notice that your doughnuts have risen a bit. Now they are ready for frying.
- Get your fryer or deep dish pan and heat up some oil to a temperature of 375 degrees Fahrenheit.
- Once your oil is hot enough, simply fry your doughnuts for about 1 min per side or until you find that all are golden in color.
- After they are fried let them sit and drain. Before eating.
- Enjoy.

Serving Size: 12 doughnuts

Timing Information:

Preparation	Cooking	Total Time
15 mins	20 mins	35 mins

Nutritional Information:

Calories	289 kcal
Carbohydrates	26.1 g
Cholesterol	32 mg
Fat	19.1 g
Fiber	0.6 g
Protein	3.5 g
Sodium	218 mg

* Percent Daily Values are based on a 2,000 calorie diet.

Doughnuts In Poland

Ingredients:

- 1 (0.6 ounce) cake compressed fresh yeast
- 3 tbsps warm water (110 degrees F/45 degrees C)
- 1 tsp white sugar
- 3 cups milk
- 3/4 cup margarine
- 5 egg yolks
- 3/4 cup white sugar
- 8 cups all-purpose flour
- 8 cups shortening for frying
- 1/4 cup white sugar

Directions

- Get a good container for mixing and combine the following: 1 tsp of sugar, water, and yeast.
- Mix these contents until they form a paste-like substance. After your mixture is paste-like you want to give it some time to rest and rise.
- While your mix is resting cook some milk and margarine, and

after your margarine has been fully cooked, let the milk and margarine mixture get to room temperature.
- Get a mixing container and you want to work the following ingredients together until you get a foamy like substance: 3/4 cup of sugar and egg yolks (mix these until they are smooth first), and cooked milk and margarine mixture.
- Combine the foamy mixture with your yeast mixture while slowly adding some flour continually and evenly, mixing until you find that everything has become thick. The idea here is: we are trying to make some dough that is fairly soft, but too much flour can make your doughnuts hard.
- Once you have made some soft dough put it to the side and let it rise until you find that the size is around double.
- Take your risen, soft dough, and make some little balls. Create as many balls as you can. Put your little doughnut balls aside and let them rise as well until you find that have doubled.

- Finally fry your little doughnut balls in shortening with a temperature of 375 degrees until everything is golden on all sides. Once golden cover the balls in sugar.
- Let everything drain and cool.
- Enjoy.

Serving Size: 3 dozen

Nutritional Information:

Calories	218 kcal
Carbohydrates	28 g
Cholesterol	30 mg
Fat	9.9 g
Fiber	0.8 g
Protein	4 g
Sodium	54 mg

* Percent Daily Values are based on a 2,000 calorie diet.

Doughnuts From Canada

Ingredients:

- 1 tbsp white sugar
- 1/2 cup warm water (110 degrees F/45 degrees C)
- 1 tbsp active dry yeast
- 1/4 cup vegetable oil
- 2 1/3 cups warm water (110 degrees F/45 degrees C)
- 1 tsp salt
- 4 tbsps white sugar
- 4 cups all-purpose flour
- 4 cups whole wheat flour
- 1 tbsp lemon juice
- 3 tbsps white sugar
- 1 tsp ground cinnamon

Directions

- To begin let's get a container and combine the following ingredients together: half of a cup of tepid water, and one tbsp of yeast and sugar. Once you have combined these ingredients put them to the side.

- Now get a big container good for mixing possibly a bowl and combine the following ingredients together: 4 tbsps of sugar, oil, salt, two and one third cups of water.
- Begin to mix these ingredients together while carefully and evenly adding yeast and flour. Combine the ingredients until you have created dough.
- You want to get a container like a bowl and cover the container with butter to coat your dough before continuing.
- Once your dough has been covered in butter cover the container and the dough with a towel and place it in a warm area like a window sill in the sun for about one and a half hours to rise.
- After the rising time has elapsed simply form your dough into little egg like shapes and flatten them to make some ovals.
- Once you have some little ovals fry them in 350 degree oil until they are all around golden.
- Remove your treats from the hot oil and cover them with: a bit of

lemon juice, white sugar, and cinnamon.
- Enjoy.

Serving Size: 3 dozen

Nutritional Information:

Calories	0 mg
Carbohydrates	23.3 g
Cholesterol	0 mg
Fat	1.9 g
Fiber	2.1 g
Protein	3.4 g
Sodium	66 mg

* Percent Daily Values are based on a 2,000 calorie diet.

Super Simple Doughnuts with Jelly

Ingredients:

- 1 cup warm milk (110 degrees F/45 degrees C)
- 1/3 cup water
- 1 egg, beaten
- 3 tbsps margarine, melted
- 3/4 cup white sugar
- 4 1/2 cups bread flour
- 1 tsp salt
- 1 1/2 tsps ground nutmeg
- 1 tbsp active dry yeast
- 3/4 cup any flavor fruit jam
- 2 quarts vegetable oil for frying

Directions

- Ok so for this recipe we need a bread machine pan. Get yours and add the following ingredients into it: yeast, milk, nutmeg, beaten egg, water, salt, melted butter, bread flour, and sugar.
- Typically a bread machine pan will have a setting for sweet

dough so set your machine for this setting and let it do its work. Once the machine has completed the work.
- Take your dough out and place it on a work surface that has been covered with flour. Let the dough sit for about ten mins.
- Flatten the dough to a sheet that has a thickness of about a quarter of an inch (1/4'). Grab a cookie cutter and make some cuts. Each cut should yield a treat of about 2 and a half inches.
- Take your cut outs and separate them. Divide them into two sets. In the middle of one set of cutouts put about half of a tsp of jam in the center.
- Wet the outside edge of each jam cutout with cold water and cover them with the other cutouts that do not have any jam. Be careful and seal the cutouts by pinching them all around.
- Set aside your cutouts and let them rise for about 45 mins to 1 hour.
- After your treats have risen fry them in hot oil that has a temperature of 375 degrees

Fahrenheit. Once the doughnuts begin to float on top of the oil you should flip them and let them continue to fry. Once fully golden on all sides remove your treats and let them drain and cool before serving.
- Add some sugar if you like.
- Enjoy.

Serving Size: 24 doughnuts

Timing Information:

Preparation	Cooking	Total Time
30 mins	20 mins	2 hrs 35 mins

Nutritional Information:

Calories	232 kcal
Carbohydrates	32.5 g
Cholesterol	9 mg
Fat	9.6 g
Fiber	0.9 g
Protein	3.9 g
Sodium	124 mg

* Percent Daily Values are based on a 2,000 calorie diet.

A Simple Doughnut of Yeast

Ingredients:

- 3 1/2 cups all-purpose flour
- 2 (.25 ounce) packages active dry yeast
- 3/4 cup milk
- 3/4 cup white sugar
- 1/4 cup butter
- 1/2 tsp salt
- 2 eggs
- 2 quarts oil for deep frying
- 1 cup confectioners' sugar for dusting

Directions

- Grab a big container good for mixing and add the following ingredients together: yeast, and 1 and 3/4 cups of flour.
- Get a pan and heat up the following items: salt, milk, butter, and sugar. Continue to let everything heat up until you find that your butter has completely melted.

- Combine your milk and melted butter mixture with the flour mixture and add your eggs as well.
- Be careful and mix everything together evenly and gradually. Get an electric mixer and on its lowest setting combine the mixture for about half a minute.
- Once you have combined the mixture for about half a min change the speed on the mixer to its highest setting and continue to combine the mixture for three mins.
- After three mins of combining the mixture you want to add more flour to it gradually while continuing to stir with a spoon to create a dough.
- Take your dough and place it on a floured place for working and knead it for a few mins (3 to 4 mins, until very soft). Put your soft dough in a container covered with oil. The dough should sit for about 1 hr in the container to rise.
- After the dough has risen take it out and flatten it on the work surface until you have created a sheet with a thickness of about

half an inch. Grab a doughnut cutting device and cut out some treats for frying.
- Put these cutouts on a sheet and cover them and let them sit and rise for about another hour.
- Now grab a pan good for frying or a deep fryer and heat some oil to 375 degrees Fahrenheit.
- Once your oil is hot simply take a batch of cutouts and fry them until golden on one side and then flip them and continue to fry until golden on the opposite side.
- After the doughnuts are fried and golden let them cool and cover them in confectioners' sugar.
- Enjoy.

Serving Size: 18 doughnuts

Timing Information:

Preparation	Cooking	Total Time
30 mins	30 mins	2 hrs 45 mins

Nutritional Information:

Calories	542 kcal
Carbohydrates	68.7 g
Cholesterol	57 mg
Fat	26.7 g
Fiber	1.6 g
Protein	7.7 g
Sodium	191 mg

* Percent Daily Values are based on a 2,000 calorie diet.

A Muffin That Is A Doughnut Too

Ingredients:

- 1/3 cup shortening
- 1 cup white sugar
- 1 egg
- 1 1/2 cups all-purpose flour
- 1 1/2 tsps baking powder
- 1/2 tsp salt
- 1/4 tsp ground cinnamon
- 1/2 cup milk
- 1/2 cup white sugar
- 1 tsp ground cinnamon

Directions

- To make this recipe we will start with our ovens, so get them heated up to a temperature of 375 degrees Fahrenheit. Get a muffin tin and cover each section with some oil, you could also line it with paper.
- Now grab a large bowl for mixing and combine the following: 1 cup of sugar, shortening, and eggs

(should be beat prior to this point).
- Combine these ingredients until you have a cream like mixture. Once you have created a cream you want to combine the following ingredients in a separate mixing container: one fourth of a tsp of cinnamon, flour, salt, and baking powder.
- Now combine both mixtures with some milk gradually and create a delicious batter. Take your batter and fill out your muffin tin with the mixture.
- Now simply enter everything into the oven for about 20 mins. If you poke a muffin with a toothpick you should find that the toothpick is clean when removed.
- As everything cooks in the oven you want to mix 1 tsp of cinnamon and half of a cup of sugar in a container.
- Let your muffins relax for a bit and cool down. But once the muffins are only slightly warm you want to cover them with the cinnamon and sugar mixture.
- Enjoy.

Serving Size: 1 dozen servings

Timing Information:

Preparation	Cooking	Total Time
10 mins	20 mins	30 mins

Nutritional Information:

Calories	216 kcal
Carbohydrates	37.7 g
Cholesterol	16 mg
Fat	6.5 g
Fiber	0.5 g
Protein	2.5 g
Sodium	152 mg

* Percent Daily Values are based on a 2,000 calorie diet.

A Doughnut From Cake Mix

Ingredients:

- 2 1/2 cups all-purpose flour
- 1/2 cup white sugar
- 1 tbsp baking powder
- 1/2 tsp salt
- 1 tsp ground cinnamon
- 1/4 tsp ground nutmeg
- 1 cup milk
- 1 egg, beaten
- 1/4 cup butter, melted and cooled
- 2 tsps vanilla extract
- 2 quarts oil for deep frying
- 1/2 tsp ground cinnamon
- 1/2 cup white sugar

Directions

- Grab a big container for mixing and combine the following: nutmeg, flour, cinnamon, half of a cup of sugar, salt, and baking powder. Once you have mixed everything together nicely you want to make an opening in the center of the mixture to put the following in: vanilla, milk, butter,

and egg. Combine until evenly mixed.
- Take this mixture and place a cover over it and place it in the frig for one hr.
- Grab a good pan for frying, possibly a deep dish skillet, or a deep fryer and get some oil to a temperature of 375 degrees Fahrenheit.
- Take out your dough from the frig and flatten it on a work surface covered in four to a thickness of half an inch.
- Use a doughnut cutting device to cut some treats out. Then take a smaller doughnut cutting device to remove holes from the treats and create doughnuts.
- Now simply take your doughnuts and fry them until golden on each side. The doughnut will float once it needs to be turned.
- Once the doughnut is fully cooked place it aside to cool and drain excess oils.
- Mix together the following as a coating for the doughnuts: half a cup of sugar, and half a cup of cinnamon.

- To coat your doughnuts place them in the same bag or container as the dry mixture and shake to get it coated.
- Enjoy.

Serving Size: 16 doughnuts and holes

Timing Information:

Preparation	Cooking	Total Time
2 hrs	15 mins	2 hrs 15 mins

Nutritional Information:

Calories	257 kcal
Carbohydrates	28.6 g
Cholesterol	20 mg
Fat	14.7 g
Fiber	0.7 g
Protein	3 g
Sodium	167 mg

* Percent Daily Values are based on a 2,000 calorie diet.

Oven Doughnuts

Ingredients:

- 1 cup white sugar
- 2 tsps baking powder
- 1 tsp baking soda
- 1 tsp ground nutmeg
- 1/2 tsp ground cloves
- 2 tsps ground cinnamon
- 3 cups all-purpose flour
- 1 cup buttermilk
- 3 eggs
- 1 tbsp honey
- 1/2 cup butter, melted

Directions

- Let's begin by getting our oven's ready.
- Set your oven to a temperature of 375 degrees Fahrenheit.
- Grab a sheet for baking or a pan for doughnuts and cover it in oil.
- Grab a container good for mixing and combine the following: flour, sugar, cinnamon, baking powder, cloves, baking soda, and nutmeg.

- Now grab another container for mixing and combine: butter, buttermilk, honey, and eggs.
- Combine these evenly and then mix them with the other container and combine everything evenly.
- Now grab a spoon and take out some of the contents and place them on the oiled sheet, to go into the oven for 12 minutes. Continue to bake until everything is cooked. You will know the treats are done when they are golden brown in color.
- Let cool. Enjoy.

Serving Size: 12 servings

Timing Information:

Preparation	Cooking	Total Time
18 mins	12 mins	30 mins

Nutritional Information:

Calories	280 kcal
Carbohydrates	43.7 g
Cholesterol	68 mg
Fat	9.5 g
Fiber	1.1 g
Protein	5.6 g
Sodium	259 mg

* Percent Daily Values are based on a 2,000 calorie diet.

Delightful Cream Based Doughnuts

Ingredients:

- 2 (.25 ounce) envelopes active dry yeast
- 1/4 cup warm water (105 to 115 degrees)
- 1 1/2 cups lukewarm milk
- 1/2 cup white sugar
- 1 tsp salt
- 2 eggs
- 1/3 cup shortening
- 5 cups all-purpose flour
- 1 quart vegetable oil for frying
- 1/3 cup butter
- 2 cups confectioners' sugar
- 1 1/2 tsps vanilla
- 4 tbsps hot water or as needed

Directions

- Grab a container and put some yeast in it. Take some tepid (warm) water and combine it with the yeast. Let this mixture sit for about five mins, and you

should eventually notice it become foamy.
- Now grab a big container good for mixing and combine the following: 2 cups of flour, the foamy yeast, shortening, milk, eggs, sugar, and eggs.
- Get an electric mixing device and set it to its lowest speed and mix everything for a few mins (2 mins). If you do not have an electric mixing device then you can also use a large spoon.
- Take your dough and put it in a container that has been covered with oil.
- Cover this container and let it stand and rest for a while. You want your dough to double in size.
- To increase the speed of the rising process you want to put the dough in a warmer location in the house, quite possibly a sunny window sill.
- Now we want to cover a working surface with some flour and flatten the dough until it has a thickness of about half an inch.
- Grab your doughnut cutting device and cut out some treats.

- Once you have cut out your doughnuts put them aside and let them rest and rise again until they are two times as big (like before with the dough) make sure the container they are in has been covered.
- Grab a pan and some butter and get the butter melted down. The heating level should be medium.
- Combine some vanilla and confectioners' sugar into the butter. This going to be our icing.
- Place this icing to the side and mix in 1 tbsp of hot water gradually until the stuff is no longer thick but of course it should not flow like water.
- Okay now you want to get your deep skillet or your fryer ready for the easiest part.
- Add some oil to your fryer and get it to a temperature of 375 degree Fahrenheit and put in your doughnuts to fry.
- Once you see a doughnut is floating and is golden flip it and get the other side nice and golden.
- Remove everything from the oil and let it cool momentarily.

- Take your doughnuts while still fairly warm and enter them into the icing for coating.
- After being coated put the doughnuts on a rack for the excess to drain off. You may want to place some wax paper under the rack to make your cleaning job easier.
- Enjoy.

Serving Size: 18 doughnuts

Timing Information:

Preparation	Cooking	Total Time
10 mins	30 mins	2 hrs 40 mins

Nutritional Information:

Calories	330 kcal
Carbohydrates	47.3 g
Cholesterol	31 mg
Fat	13.4 g
Fiber	1.1 g
Protein	5.3 g
Sodium	171 mg

* Percent Daily Values are based on a 2,000 calorie diet.

A Jelly Cupcake Doughnut

Ingredients:

- cooking spray
- 1 (18.5 ounce) package yellow cake mix
- 1 (3.5 ounce) package instant French vanilla pudding mix
- 1 cup whole milk
- 1 cup vegetable oil
- 4 eggs
- 1 (12 ounce) jar seedless raspberry jam
- 2 tbsps confectioners' sugar for dusting

Directions

- Let's begin by getting our oven nice and hot to 350 degrees Fahrenheit.
- Grab your muffin tin and coat it with oil or some non-stick spray and put paper liners into each cup.
- Now get a big bowl for mixing combine the following: eggs,

yellow cake mix, milk, and some French vanilla pudding.
- You will most likely want to use an electric mixing device for this. After mixing there should be no dry areas.
- You should then proceed to scrape the container and mix again for a few mins.
- Take your mixture and fill out each muffin section to its half-way mark.
- Put the muffin container into the oven for 20 mins and everything should be nice and golden.
- Take out your muffins and allow them to rest and cool off a bit.
- Now finally before serving you want to cut into each muffin about 1 inch deep and three fourths of an inch wide. Fill this opening in each muffin with raspberry jam.
- Cover your cupcakes with some confectioners' sugar.
- Enjoy.

Serving Size: 2 dozen cupcakes

Timing Information:

Preparation	Cooking	Total Time
30 mins	20 mins	1 hr 20 mins

Nutritional Information:

Calories	246 kcal
Carbohydrates	31 g
Cholesterol	32 mg
Fat	12.9 g
Fiber	0.2 g
Protein	2.3 g
Sodium	216 mg

* Percent Daily Values are based on a 2,000 calorie diet.

Doughnuts from Greenland

Ingredients:

- 8 eggs
- 1 quart buttermilk
- 1/4 cup melted butter
- 4 cups all-purpose flour
- 1 tsp salt
- 2 tbsps white sugar
- 1 tsp baking soda
- 1 1/2 tbsps ground cardamom
- 2 cups vegetable shortening, melted

Directions

- For this recipe we need specific type of pan called an Aebleskiver pan these are usually electric and will make our job much easier.
- Get your Aebleskiver pan nice and hot and combine the following ingredients in a large mixing container: butter, eggs, and buttermilk.
- Continue to combine the following into the egg mixture slowly and evenly: cardamom,

flour, sugar, and salt and make sure everything is nice and smooth.
- In each cup of your Aebleskiver pan you want to put about one tbsp of shortening for extra taste.
- Make sure everything gets nice and heated before continuing.
- 75% of each cup in the Aebleskiver pan should be filled with your batter.
- Let everything cook for about 4 mins.
- Then give each section a quarter of a turn.
- The point is to get the remaining batter to fall to the bottom to be cooked.
- Simply continue turning and cooking until you have a nice golden ball.
- Let everything cool and enjoy.

Serving Size: 48 servings

Timing Information:

Preparation	Cooking	Total Time
10 mins	45 mins	55 mins

Nutritional Information:

Calories	145 kcal
Carbohydrates	9.6 g
Cholesterol	34 mg
Fat	10.6 g
Fiber	0.3 g
Protein	2.8 g
Sodium	115 mg

* Percent Daily Values are based on a 2,000 calorie diet.

A Strawberry Shortcake Sweet Doughnut

Ingredients:

- 2 cups heavy whipping cream
- 1/2 cup confectioners' sugar
- 1 tsp vanilla extract
- 4 glazed doughnuts, halved horizontally
- 1 quart strawberries, hulled and sliced

Directions

- Grab a large container for mixing possibly a metal bowl and combine the following: vanilla extract, cream, and sugar.
- With an electric mixing device you want to mix everything until a peak forms.
- Take one doughnut and cut it in half.
- Put the bottom portion of the cut doughnut on a plate. Take a quarter of a cup of whipped cream and cover the plated doughnut with it.

- Now you want to take about a quarter of a cup of strawberries and cover the whipped cream and make another layer of both (whipped cream and then strawberries).
- Take the other half of the doughnut and place it on top to make a delicious sandwich. Make as many as you like.
- Enjoy.

Serving Size: 4 servings

Timing Information:

Preparation	Cooking	Total Time
15 mins		15 mins

Nutritional Information:

Calories	766 kcal
Carbohydrates	57.4 g
Cholesterol	167 mg
Fat	58.2 g
Fiber	3.8 g
Protein	7.3 g
Sodium	252 mg

* Percent Daily Values are based on a 2,000 calorie diet.

Jelly Doughnut II

Ingredients:

- 3 eggs, beaten
- 1/2 cup milk
- 1/2 tsp vanilla extract
- 1/4 cup sugar
- 1 cup all-purpose flour
- 1/2 tsp baking powder
- 1/4 tsp salt
- canola oil
- 10 slices white bread
- strawberry (or any flavor) jam
- confectioners' sugar

Directions

- Grab a nice container for mixing and combine the following ingredients: sugar, eggs, vanilla, and milk.
- Take care to mix or blend everything together until you have a nice smooth mixture with dissolved sugar.
- Grab another mixing container and combine salt, flour, and

baking powder together and mix it all up evenly.
- Now get a pot good for frying or a deep skillet and get your oil to a temperature of 375 degrees Fahrenheit.
- Take your white bread slices and trim off the crusts.
- Make sandwiches with the jam.
- Slice each sandwich in half and cover it with the egg mixture by submerging each piece for a second or two.
- Simply fry your jelly sandwiches in batches for about 3 minutes. After 3 mins of frying you should notice them getting puffy and becoming golden.
- Remove them from the hot oil and remove excess oil with a paper towel.
- Cover everything with confectioner's sugar.
- Enjoy.

Serving Size: 40 doughnuts

Timing Information:

Preparation	Cooking	Total Time
20 mins	20 mins	40 mins

Nutritional Information:

Calories	263 kcal
Carbohydrates	13.4 g
Cholesterol	14 mg
Fat	23.1 g
Fiber	0.3 g
Protein	1.4 g
Sodium	70 mg

* Percent Daily Values are based on a 2,000 calorie diet.

Doughnut Ice Cream

Ingredients:

- 3 day-old glazed doughnuts, cut into 8 pieces
- 1 cup cold, strong, brewed coffee
- 1/2 cup sugar
- 2 cups heavy cream
- 1 (14 ounce) can sweetened condensed milk
- 1/2 cup milk
- 1 tsp vanilla extract

Directions

- Grab a non-deep container and put inside the container your pieces of glazed doughnuts.
- Take your coffee and pour it on top of the doughnuts but only pour enough so that the doughnuts can absorb the coffee fully. Now freeze these soaked doughnuts.
- Now take the rest of the coffee and combine it with the following in a large container good for

mixing: sweetened condensed milk, vanilla, sugar, normal milk, and cream, mix it all together evenly.
- Now take the second coffee mixture and put it in an ice cream maker and let the machine turn everything into ice cream.
- Take your frozen doughnuts from the freezer and put into the ice cream and mix it all evenly.
- Put everything into a new container that can be stored and covered and place the covered container in the freezer for about 12 hours.
- Enjoy.

Serving Size: 1 quart

Timing Information:

Preparation	Cooking	Total Time
20 mins		14 hrs 20 mins

Nutritional Information:

Calories	511 kcal
Carbohydrates	51.6 g
Cholesterol	101 mg
Fat	31.7 g
Fiber	0.3 g
Protein	7.1 g
Sodium	169 mg

* Percent Daily Values are based on a 2,000 calorie diet.

Bread Pudding Doughnuts Re-Imagined

Ingredients:

- 4 stale raised glazed donuts
- 1/2 cup raisins or other dried fruit
- 2 eggs (room temperature)
- 1 (12 fluid ounce) can evaporated milk
- 2 tbsps white sugar (optional)
- 1 tsp vanilla extract
- 1/4 tsp almond extract (optional)
- 1 tsp grated orange zest
- 2 tsps ground cinnamon
- 1/4 tsp ground nutmeg

Directions

- Let's begin this recipe by getting our oven's ready, set your oven to a temperature of 350 degrees Fahrenheit.
- Grab a smaller dish for baking and coat it with oil.
- Take your doughnuts and break them into small nice sized pieces.

- Mix together raisins and doughnut pieces in the oiled dish.
- Get a mixing container and an electric mixing device and mix the following items: almond extract, eggs, vanilla extract, evaporated milk, nutmeg, cinnamon, and sugar.
- Take this liquid mixture and cover the donut pieces with it. Apply some pressure to the doughnuts so the milk is absorbed.
- For about 15 mins let everything stand.
- Grab a larger dish for baking and place the smaller dish inside the larger dish.
- Put water inside the larger dish until it reaches the halfway mark of the smaller dish.
- Simply bake the dishes for 40 mins.
- Let cool.
- Enjoy.

Serving Size: 6 servings

Timing Information:

Preparation	Cooking	Total Time
15 mins	45 mins	1 hr 15 mins

Nutritional Information:

Calories	329 kcal
Carbohydrates	44.3 g
Cholesterol	80 mg
Fat	13.6 g
Fiber	1.9 g
Protein	9.5 g
Sodium	311 mg

* Percent Daily Values are based on a 2,000 calorie diet.

Herman Doughnuts II

Ingredients:

Serving Size: 12 doughnuts

- 8 cups vegetable oil for frying
- 1/2 tsp baking soda
- 1 tbsp water
- 2 tbsps shortening
- 1/2 cup white sugar
- 2 egg yolks
- 1/2 cup Herman Sourdough Starter
- 1/4 cup buttermilk
- 1/2 tsp vanilla extract
- 1/2 cup applesauce
- 1/2 tsp ground cinnamon
- 1/2 tsp ground nutmeg
- 1 1/2 tsps baking powder
- 2 3/4 cups all-purpose flour

Directions

- Get a deep dish skillet or a general pan good for frying and get some oil to a temperature of 375 degrees Fahrenheit.

- Grab a small container for mixing and put some tepid water and baking soda. Let the baking soda dissolve in the water.
- Grab a large mixing container and evenly combine the following ingredients: dissolved baking soda, egg yolks, applesauce, Herman sour dough starter, vanilla extract, and buttermilk.
- In a separate container mix flour, cinnamon, baking powder, and nutmeg.
- Carefully stir in your dry ingredients with your wet ingredients and make some dough.
- Create a nice working surface by layering some flour on the counter and flattening your dough to a thickness of 3/4 of an inch.
- Use a doughnut cutter to cut out some doughnuts and leave them alone for about 10 mins to rest.
- Simply take your doughnuts and fry them until golden brown on both sides.
- Remove excess oils and serve hot.

Serving Size: 12 doughnuts

Timing Information:

Preparation	Cooking	Total Time
10 mins	30 mins	50 mins

Nutritional Information:

Calories	302 kcal
Carbohydrates	32 g
Cholesterol	34 mg
Fat	17.9 g
Fiber	1 g
Protein	3.6 g
Sodium	121 mg

* Percent Daily Values are based on a 2,000 calorie diet.

Classical Doughnuts with Apple Cider

Ingredients:

Doughnuts:

- 1 cup apple cider
- 1 cup white sugar
- 1/4 cup butter, at room temperature
- 2 eggs
- 1/2 cup buttermilk
- 3 1/2 cups all-purpose flour, or more as needed
- 2 tsps baking powder
- 1 tsp baking soda
- 1/2 tsp ground cinnamon
- 1/2 tsp salt
- 1/8 tsp ground nutmeg
- 2 cups vegetable oil for frying, or as needed

Glaze:

- 1 cup confectioners' sugar
- 2 tbsps apple cider

Directions

- Grab your favorite pot for boiling and get about 1 cup of apple cider to a state of boiling.
- Continue to boil this cider down until your 1 cup has turned to 1/4 of a cup. In general this will take around 10 mins.
- Let the boiling pot and its mixture cool down to room temperature
- Get a container for mixing and an electric mixing device and mix the following until it becomes like a cream: butter and white sugar.
- Now combine with your creamy mixture some eggs one by one. Your eggs should be beaten before they are entered into the creamy mixture.
- Now combine the room temperature cider, and buttermilk into this as well.
- Grab another mixing container and combine the following dry ingredients: nutmeg, flour, salt, baking powder, cinnamon, and baking soda.
- Now mix together your dry and wet ingredients in a steady and

gradual manner to create some nice pliable dough.
- Get your work surface ready by covering it with flour and flatten your dough into a sheet that is about half an inch in thickness.
- Get a frying pot, filled with oil and get it nice and hot (350 to 375 degrees).
- Fry your doughnuts in batches until golden brown.
- While your doughnuts are frying or before you begin frying. Mix some confectioner's sugar and some apple cider together to make a glaze coating for the doughnuts and set it aside.
- Once all the doughnuts are fried and have had their excess oils removed glaze them while warm.
- Enjoy.

Serving Size: 12 servings

Timing Information:

Preparation	Cooking	Total Time
30 mins	20 mins	1 hr 20 mins

Nutritional Information:

Calories	333 kcal
Carbohydrates	58.9 g
Cholesterol	42 mg
Fat	8.8 g
Fiber	1 g
Protein	5.2 g
Sodium	336 mg

* Percent Daily Values are based on a 2,000 calorie diet.

Oven Doughnuts II

Ingredients:

Doughnuts:
- 2 cups baking mix (such as Bisquick ®)
- 1/3 cup milk
- 1 egg
- 2 tbsps white sugar
- 1/8 tsp ground cinnamon

Coating:

- 1/4 cup butter, melted
- 1/2 cup white sugar

Directions

- Let's begin this recipe by getting our ovens hot and to a temperature of 400 degrees Fahrenheit
- Get a nice sized container for mixing and combine the following ingredients: cinnamon, two tbsps of sugar, baking mix, eggs, and milk.

- Mix everything together evenly until you have a nice soft dough.
- Place some flour on a surface for working and flatten your dough out into a sheet that is half an inch thick. Use your doughnut cutting device to make some cutouts.
- Put all the doughnuts on a baking sheet and put them in the oven until they are fully cooked and only lightly brown this should take about 9 minutes of baking.
- Now to make your coating you want to mix some sugar and melted butter together until you have a glaze and cover the doughnuts with this.
- Enjoy.

Serving Size: 16 servings

Timing Information:

Preparation	Cooking	Total Time
15 mins	10 mins	25 mins

Nutritional Information:

Calories	124 kcal
Carbohydrates	17.3 g
Cholesterol	20 mg
Fat	5.6 g
Fiber	0.3 g
Protein	1.7 g
Sodium	216 mg

* Percent Daily Values are based on a 2,000 calorie diet.

Classical Doughnuts with Apple Cider II

Ingredients:

Doughnuts:

- 3 1/4 cups all-purpose flour, or more if needed (divided)
- 2 envelopes Fleischmann's® RapidRise Yeast
- 2 tbsps sugar
- 1 tsp salt
- 1 tsp Spice Islands® Ground Saigon Cinnamon
- 1 cup milk plus
- 2 tbsps milk
- 1/4 cup butter or margarine
- 3 egg yolks
- Mazola® Corn Oil for deep frying

Apple Cider Glaze:

- 1 cup apple cider
- 2 cups powdered sugar
- 1 tbsp Karo® Light Corn Syrup

Directions

- Get a larger sized container for mixing and mix the following ingredients together evenly: cinnamon, 2 cups of flour, salt, undissolved yeast, salt, and sugar.
- Now you want to heat some milk and butter until everything is nice and melted.
- Combine this with a mixture of egg yolks and the dry flour mix.
- Using a low speed mixer, mix everything until you form dough.
- Place the dough in a container and let it sit for 10 mins.
- On a flour covered surface flatten the dough to a sheet with a thickness of half an inch.
- Grab your doughnut cutter and make some cutouts.
- Use your finger to poke a hole in each doughnut.
- Put everything on an oiled sheet for baking and let it all sit for about 45 mins to rise bit more.
- Heat up some oil in a deep skillet to 375 degrees Fahrenheit and fry your doughnuts until golden on both sides.
- This will occur in about 3 mins.

- Serve the plain doughnuts with the apple cider mixture mentioned in last recipe.
- Enjoy.

Serving Size: 15 doughnuts

Timing Information:

Preparation	Cooking	Total Time
35 mins	15 mins	1 hr 50 mins

Nutritional Information:

Calories	293 kcal
Carbohydrates	43 g
Cholesterol	51 mg
Fat	12.1 g
Fiber	0.8 g
Protein	4 g
Sodium	191 mg

* Percent Daily Values are based on a 2,000 calorie diet.

DOUGHNUTS IN THE NETHERLANDS

Ingredients:

- 1 (0.6 ounce) cake compressed fresh yeast
- 1 cup lukewarm milk
- 2 1/4 cups all-purpose flour
- 2 tsps salt
- 1 egg
- 3/4 cup dried currants
- 3/4 cup raisins
- 1 Granny Smith apple - peeled, cored and finely chopped
- 1 quart vegetable oil for deep-frying
- 1 cup confectioners' sugar for dusting

Directions

- Take your yeast and combine it with some milk that has been warmed.
- You want to make sure that the yeast has fully dissolved in the milk by letting everything stand.

- Grab a sifter and combine some salt and flour with it in a large container good for mixing.
- Now you want to add the following ingredients and mix evenly to make a nice batter: yeast and milk mix, and eggs.
- Finally after you have created the batter. Mix in your currants, apples, and raisins.
- Place a towel over this container and set it to the side and let the contents rise. Wait about one hr for everything to increase in size.
- Get a deep dish skillet or deep fryer and heat oil to 375 degrees Fahrenheit and begin to fry some dough balls that you can easily make by removing a spoonful of dough.
- Let the dough balls cook for about 8 mins and become golden all over.
- Remove them from the oil and remove the excess with paper towels and finally cover them with confectioner's sugar.
- Enjoy.

Serving Size: 1 dozen

Timing Information:

Preparation	Cooking	Total Time
2 hrs	8 mins	2 hrs 8 mins

Nutritional Information:

Calories	270 kcal
Carbohydrates	45.8 g
Cholesterol	17 mg
Fat	8.5 g
Fiber	2 g
Protein	4.5 g
Sodium	405 mg

* Percent Daily Values are based on a 2,000 calorie diet.

Doughnuts for Autumn

(Maple and Pumpkin)

Ingredients:

- 1 tsp vegetable oil, or as needed
- 1 cup all-purpose flour
- 1 tsp baking powder
- 3/4 tsp ground cinnamon
- 1/2 tsp ground ginger
- 1/4 tsp ground nutmeg
- 1/4 tsp ground allspice
- 1/4 tsp salt
- 1/8 tsp ground cloves
- 1/4 cup light brown sugar
- 3/4 cup pumpkin puree
- 1/3 cup vegetable oil
- 1/3 cup maple syrup
- 1/4 cup buttermilk
- 1 large egg
- 1/2 cup confectioners' sugar
- 3 tbsps maple syrup
- 1/4 cup finely chopped roasted pumpkin seeds

Directions

- Let's begin this recipe by getting our oven hot to a temperature of 375 degrees Fahrenheit.
- Get a pan for the doughnuts and coat it with oil.
- Grab your sifter and combine the following in a container for mixing: cloves, baking powder, salt, cinnamon, allspice, nutmeg, and ginger as well as flour and brown sugar.
- Now take your puree of pumpkin and the following ingredients and mix them in a big container: eggs, one third cup of veggie oil, buttermilk, and one third cup of maple syrup.
- Take both mixtures and combine them into a batter.
- Put this batter in the frig for 40 mins.
- If using a doughnut pan place one fourth of a cup of batter into each section.
- Baking time for this dish is about 13 mins.
- Finally to make the topping for the doughnuts combine maple syrup and confectioners' sugar

until it becomes a glaze and cover the doughnuts with this.
- Enjoy.

Serving Size: 8 servings

Timing Information:

Preparation	Cooking	Total Time
40 mins	10 mins	50 mins

Nutritional Information:

Calories	275 kcal
Carbohydrates	41.9 g
Cholesterol	24 mg
Fat	11.1 g
Fiber	1.3 g
Protein	3.3 g
Sodium	210 mg

* Percent Daily Values are based on a 2,000 calorie diet.

Printed in Great Britain
by Amazon